THE TIME~TRAVELING TWINS
Roughing It *on the* Oregon Trail

D0817615

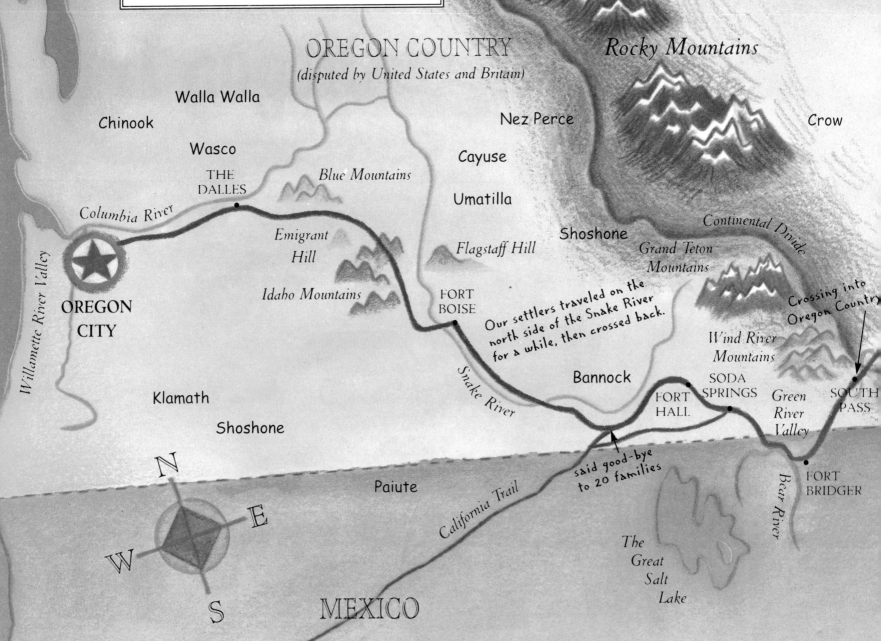

OREGON TRAIL, 1843

OREGON COUNTRY
(disputed by United States and Britain)

Rocky Mountains

Walla Walla

Chinook

Nez Perce

Crow

Wasco

Cayuse

THE DALLES

Blue Mountains

Umatilla

Columbia River

Continental Divide

Shoshone

Grand Teton Mountains

Emigrant Hill

Flagstaff Hill

Idaho Mountains

FORT BOISE

Our settlers traveled on the north side of the Snake River for a while, then crossed back.

Crossing into Oregon Country

Willamette River Valley

Wind River Mountains

OREGON CITY

Bannock

SODA SPRINGS

Green River Valley

SOUTH PASS

Klamath

Snake River

FORT HALL

Shoshone

said good-bye to 20 families

Bear River

FORT BRIDGER

N

E

Paiute

California Trail

W

S

The Great Salt Lake

MEXICO

UNITED STATES TERRITORIES

Great Plains

Northern Cheyenne

Arapaho

Just about halfway there!

Sweetwater River

FORT LARAMIE

met Indians

SCOTT'S BLUFF

COURT-HOUSE ROCK

saw buffalo

Platte River

Lakota Sioux

Oto

Kansa

Kickapoo

Potawatomi

Missouri River

wrote our names

CHIMNEY ROCK

INDEPENDENCE ROCK

tough river crossing

Arapaho

Pawnee

UNITED STATES

Southern Cheyenne

Great Plains

The Oregon Trail

INDEPENDENCE, MISSOURI

Ute

Continental Divide

Rocky Mountains

CANADA

OREGON COUNTRY

LOUISIANA PURCHASE

MEXICO

UNITED STATES OF AMERICA

REPUBLIC OF TEXAS

The locations of many Native American tribes are noted on this map. That doesn't mean the tribes always stayed in one area, though. They moved from place to place, so that it was not unusual for the wagon train to meet Crow in a region mostly populated by Cheyenne.

To Joyanne Bates, Master Teacher and Travelin' Gal
–D.S.

To my fellow trailmates Chris, Izzy and Gwen and the Bentonite Cowboy
–H.B.

No part of this publication may be reproduced in whole or in part, or stored in a retrieval system, or transmitted in any form or by any means, electronic, mechanical, photocopying, recording, or otherwise, without written permission of the publisher. For information regarding permission, write to Joanna Cotler Books, an imprint of HarperCollins Publishers, 10 East 53rd Street, New York, NY 10022.

ISBN 0-439-32763-6

Text copyright © 2000 by Diane Stanley. Illustrations copyright © 2000 by Holly Berry. All rights reserved. Published by Scholastic Inc., 555 Broadway, New York, NY 10012, by arrangement with Joanna Cotler Books, an imprint of HarperCollins Publishers. SCHOLASTIC and associated logos are trademarks and/or registered trademarks of Scholastic Inc.

12 11 10 9 8 7 6 5 4 3   2 3 4 5 6 7/0

Printed in the U.S.A.   08

First Scholastic printing, January 2002

Typography by Alicia Mikles

◆ THE TIME~TRAVELING TWINS ◆
Roughing It *on the* Oregon Trail

Diane Stanley

by D I A N E   S T A N L E Y   *Illustrated by* H O L L Y   B E R R Y

SCHOLASTIC INC.

New York Toronto London Auckland Sydney
Mexico City New Delhi Hong Kong Buenos Aires

Our parents were going on a two-week trip to Paris,
where you have to sit politely through long meals
and be very well behaved in the hotel.
That was why we went to stay with Grandma.
Now, she's not like any other grandmother we know.
She's always studying up on our ancestors,
and her walls are covered with portraits
of people who lived long, long ago.
As if this weren't weird enough, imagine our surprise
when, right after our parents left,
Grandma asked us which one of our
ancestors we'd like to visit!

You mean
I could actually
meet that guy?

We decided to visit our
great-great-great-great-grandmother Elizabeth.
But first we had to change our clothes.
Grandma said we couldn't go out west in 1843
wearing shorts and T-shirts.

When we were finally ready, Grandma put on her magic hat. Then we all held hands and closed our eyes and waited. Suddenly we felt very strange. . . .

When we opened our eyes, things had really changed.

Pretty soon we found the wagon we were looking for. Walking beside it was our great-great-great-great-grandmother Elizabeth. Of course, in 1843, she was only ten years old. Grandma told Elizabeth's family that we were distant relatives and we didn't have a wagon. They said we could ride with them.

Usually we walked.
If we got really tired, though,
we rode in the wagon.
It was crowded and very bumpy.
You couldn't see much.

Yow!
This thing needs
shock absorbers!

It is pretty rough. But that's not surprising, since there isn't really any road here—just a few wagon ruts. And, of course, the wheels have iron "tires"! But you might as well get used to it, dear, because it's going to get a whole lot worse.

Late in the afternoon, the caravan stopped.
The men unhitched the animals and put them out to graze.
The children helped the women get ready to make supper.
They gathered wood for the family cookfire and went to the river
to get water. If they had cows, they milked them.
We sat on the ground to eat our dinner of bacon and beans.

What made you decide to leave your home and move out west?

Like lots of folks, we lost our farm in the Panic of 1837. But out west there's free land and a chance to start over. We've been saving up for six years now to buy the wagon and the oxen and all our supplies.

The Panic of 1837 was what we'd call a depression.

Later, while we were scouring the pots and washing the dishes,
Elizabeth's mother mixed some dried beans with water and a little bacon.
Then she dug a hole, filled it with hot coals, and put the bean pot in it.
The beans would cook slowly overnight, she said.
All she'd have to do the next day was heat them up for dinner.

Want to go bark at the cattle?

But it had been a long day, and another long day lay ahead.
After a while, the music stopped,
and people crawled into their tents or wagons for the night.
Everyone, that is, but the men whose turn it was
to keep watch over the cattle and the wagon train.
It must have been a spooky job, out here in the wilderness,
under the stars, listening to the wolves howl.
As for us—we went right to sleep.

The next morning, while it was still dark,
we heard the sentries yell, "Turn out! Turn out!"
That meant it was time to get up.
We had slept in our clothes,
so all we had to do was put our shoes on.
Then everybody got to work.
The women cooked slam-johns and sowbelly—
that means pancakes and bacon.
The men rounded up the cattle and
hitched the oxen to the wagons.
The tents were packed away and the dishes washed.
By about six o'clock, just as the sun rose,
the sound of bugles told everybody
it was time to hit the trail.

Life on the Oregon Trail was pretty much the same, day after day: hot and very, very dusty. Because of all the dust, everybody wanted their wagon to be up front. To be fair to all the families, whoever got to be in front one day went to the rear the next. That way, nobody argued about it. Soon we came to a wide, muddy river called the Platte and followed it, going west.

Then one great day we saw our first herd of buffalo.
We could see them off in the distance, raising a great cloud of dust.
You could feel the ground tremble as they passed.
Men grabbed their guns and powder horns and rode off after them.
It meant we would have fresh meat.
I don't think anybody dreamed that in a few years
there would hardly be any buffalo left.

Sometimes we had to cross rivers.
If there was a shallow section, we just drove across.
After all, the wagons were pretty high.
But some rivers were too deep to ford,
so we wrapped the wagons in buffalo hides
and coated them with tallow and ashes.
This made them waterproof.
We took the wheels off the wagons and
floated them across like boats. The animals had to swim.
You needed to be careful with the mules, though.
If they got water in their ears, they might go into a panic and drown.
But all our animals made it just fine.

After a while the trail got rougher.
It was hot, and we were tortured by sand flies and mosquitoes.
The animals suffered too, grunting and flicking their tails to drive them away.
The trail began to slope upward, toward the mountains.
We passed landmarks such as Courthouse Rock and Chimney Rock,
named by the trappers who passed there in the 1820s.
We were just past Scott's Bluff when word was passed down the line
of wagons that the pilot had seen signs of Indians.

We stopped by a spring at midday.
For "nooning," we never took the time to make fires and cook.
We ate cold beans and biscuits while the animals grazed and rested.
All at once everyone stopped talking—Indians were approaching.
We watched as they rode peacefully into our camp, then got down
from their horses. The leader asked to see our "chief," so the pilot
came forward and they shook hands. The Indian who spoke was a
Crow chief named Yellow Feather. He sat down in a circle with
our pilot and some other men and took out his red clay pipe.
They mixed tobacco with red willow bark, and took turns smoking it.
The pilot offered them some dried buffalo meat.
After a while they shook hands again, and the Indians went away.

Finally we reached Fort Laramie and set up camp nearby.
It wasn't a military fort—the nearest soldiers were back in the United States,
seven hundred miles to the east.
Fort Laramie was a trading center, where we could buy supplies,
repair wagons, get horses shod, and rest.
We had been gone forty days and still had a long way to go.

When we headed back out on the trail, things got even harder.
The wind swept endlessly across the prairie, and the nights were cold.
There was hardly even any sagebrush for our cookfires.
We had to burn buffalo chips instead.

We stopped at a place called Independence Rock.
People called it the "register" of the Oregon Trail.
We mixed grease and gunpowder to make paint and
wrote our names on the rock beside all the other names
of people who had been there before us.

The trail got even rougher as we climbed the rocky slope of the Wind River Mountains.
At last we reached the top at South Pass, and crossed the Continental Divide.
That's the point where all the rivers start to flow west instead of east.
Then the trail led us back down the slope and into Oregon country.
We stopped for the night in the beautiful Green River valley.
It had once been full of beaver, but even in 1843 there are scarcely any left.
They had been caught by trappers and turned into gentlemen's top hats.

Before heading up into the Grand Teton mountains,
we rested in the lush meadows near the Bear River.
We ate fresh trout and elk with wild onions.
There were even berries for dessert.
Later we stopped at Soda Springs,

where the water came out all bubbly
and tickled your nose when you drank it.
At Fort Hall we said good-bye to about twenty families.
They turned off to the southwest,
following the California Trail to San Francisco.

Then came the rain.
For three days we were wet to the skin,
and we couldn't make a fire in all that time.
The wagons slipped around in the mud,
making them harder for the oxen to pull.

We all had to get out and walk, up to our ankles in mud.
Everybody was so tired and hungry
by the time we reached the mountains
that some were near despair.

As we went higher, it grew cold and began to snow,
even though it was only September.
The slopes on the other side were so steep,
we had to ease the wagons down on ropes anchored to trees.
But by then, lots of people didn't have wagons anymore.

At last we reached the Columbia River.
From there you could travel by raft
to the lush Willamette River valley.
Though that would be the end of the journey,
starting a new life wouldn't be easy for Elizabeth's family.
They had to cut down trees to build a cabin before winter,
and they needed to clear fields of rocks and brush
for planting crops in the spring.
It was the end of the trail for us, too—time to go home.
We hated to say good-bye,
knowing we'd never see them again.

We made it—and what beautiful country! I just know we'll build a good life here!

Boy, we sure had some adventures together!

I'll miss you so much!

Sniff!

When the last boat was out of sight,
we stood there on the riverbank for a while.
Then Grandma put on her hat, and we all
held hands and closed our eyes and waited.
Everything happened just like before,
and we were back at Grandma's.

Grandma, what happened to them all?

Well, Jed took over the farm after his father died. He married that red-haired girl named Cora—remember her?—and they had three children. Martha grew up to be a teacher, helping a whole generation of young Americans learn to read and write in a little one-room schoolhouse. As for Elizabeth, she eventually married a kindhearted rancher named James who came down the Oregon Trail in the summer of 1844, and they had six children. Their third daughter, Sofia, was my great-grandmother.

I'm so glad it all turned out OK.

I remember Cora. She had the little spotted dog with the beautiful eyes.

When Mom and Dad came to pick us up,
they told us all about their trip to Paris.
They said it had been a great adventure.
We thought that was pretty funny!
But we just winked at Grandma and didn't say a word.
We know how to keep a secret.

When it was time to leave, Grandma handed us each a present.

ELIZABETH
1843
HOME
SWEET
HOME

POETRY
by

Dear Liz and Lenny,
    This is so you will
always remember
Elizabeth and Jed and
Martha—and their great
trek on the Oregon Trail.
And now, my little
pioneers—where shall
we go next?
                Love,
                Grandma

AUTHOR'S NOTE

The story of Liz and Lenny along the Oregon Trail shows only one small part of a very big picture, an epic clash of two very different cultures. The European settlers who came to the Americas firmly believed that any land that was not formally parceled off as belonging to some state or individual—with a legal document to prove it—was up for grabs. So grab they did. Many different nations—including Britain, France, Spain, Mexico, Russia, and the United States—claimed to "own" certain parts of the land on the American continent. The Native American peoples, who had been living there all along, were particularly vulnerable to this land grab because their many nations were not united, nor as well armed, and because they didn't believe in "owning" land—they thought it belonged to the earth and all who lived on it.

It is all history now, complete with its rights and wrongs. The best we can do is try to understand what happened and why.

—D.S.

The Oregon Trail stretches 2,170 miles from the Missouri River to the Willamette River, and was traveled by over 400,000 settlers between 1840 and 1880. Three hundred miles of trails are still discernible today, and an auto route can be followed from Independence, Missouri, to Oregon City, Oregon.

For more information about the trail, contact:
Oregon National Historic Trail ❋ National Park Service
Long Distance Trails Office ❋ 324 South State Street ❋ Suite 250
P.O. Box 45155 ❋ Salt Lake City, UT 84145-0155

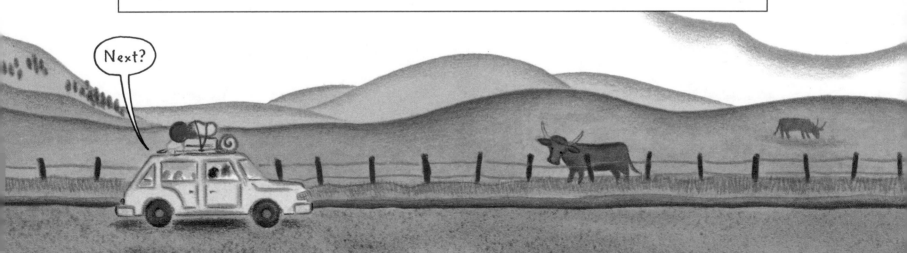

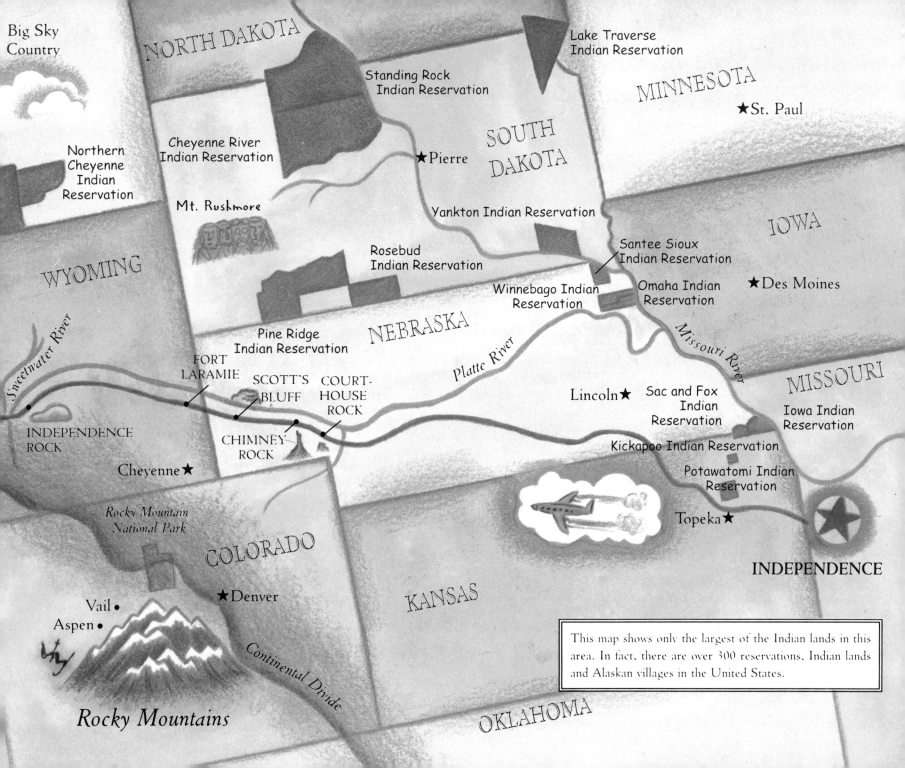

Big Sky
Country

NORTH DAKOTA

Lake Traverse
Indian Reservation

Standing Rock
Indian Reservation

MINNESOTA

★ St. Paul

Cheyenne River
Indian Reservation

★ Pierre

SOUTH
DAKOTA

Northern
Cheyenne
Indian
Reservation

Mt. Rushmore

Yankton Indian Reservation

IOWA

Rosebud
Indian Reservation

Santee Sioux
Indian Reservation

★ Des Moines

WYOMING

Winnebago Indian
Reservation

Omaha Indian
Reservation

Pine Ridge
Indian Reservation

NEBRASKA

Sweetwater River

FORT
LARAMIE

SCOTT'S
BLUFF

COURT-
HOUSE
ROCK

Platte River

Missouri River

MISSOURI

INDEPENDENCE
ROCK

CHIMNEY
ROCK

Lincoln ★

Sac and Fox
Indian
Reservation

Iowa Indian
Reservation

Cheyenne ★

Kickapoo Indian Reservation

Rocky Mountain
National Park

Potawatomi Indian
Reservation

COLORADO

Topeka ★

INDEPENDENCE

★ Denver

Vail •

KANSAS

Aspen •

Continental Divide

Rocky Mountains

OKLAHOMA

This map shows only the largest of the Indian lands in this
area. In fact, there are over 300 reservations, Indian lands
and Alaskan villages in the United States.